Saving Money on Editing & Choosing the Best Editor: An Indie Author Guide

by

Janell E. Robisch

Saving Money on Editing & Choosing the Best Editor: An Indie Author Guide

Copyright © 2017 by Janell E. Robisch

Published by Mistweave Press 2017

Printed in the United States of America

First Printing, 2017

Mistweave Press, P.O. Box 691, Luray, VA 22835

Cover design by Janell E. Robisch

Contents

1. The Value of Patience..1

   How Patience Affects Your Editing Costs 3

2. Self-Editing 9

   How to Make the Most of Self-Editing............11

   Tips for Self-Editing 12

   Other Resources for Self-Editing....................16

3. Using Readers 19

   Why You Need Readers....................................19

   What Kinds of Readers Do You Need? 20

      Alpha Readers 21

      Beta Readers...22

      Critique Partners...23

      Critique Groups...23

   Where to Find Readers 24

      Critique Groups and Partners.....................24

      Alpha and Beta Readers.............................24

   Resources 25

4. Using Editing Tools..27

   What about the Costs?.......................................29

   Notable Editing Tools 29

Word Add-Ons..30

Stand-Alone and Multi-Integrating Tools.................32

5. Final Tips..35

Improve Your Own Skills................................... 35

Practice Smart Shopping.................................. 38

A Note on Cheap Editing.................................. 40

6. Finding Your Best Editor................................43

Before You Start Vetting................................. 44

Education 46

Relevant Experience 47

Process... 49

Professionalism 50

Internet/Social Media Presence......................... 51

Past Clients... 52

Sample the Service..................................... 53

Upfront Payments....................................... 53

Thanks 54

Note from the Author 57

Free Self-Editing Checklist for Your First Draft............ 57

About the Author 59

Where to Find Janell Online 60

Acknowledgments 61

Saving Money on Editing & Choosing the Best Editor: An Indie Author Guide

by

Janell E. Robisch

1. The Value of Patience

Congratulations, you've written a book! Now, according to conventional wisdom, whether you are planning to self-publish your book or submit it for publication through a traditional publisher, you need to have your book edited. The editing process, a series of several steps that includes structural editing, copyediting, and proofreading, will transform your book from a rough draft into a polished work that you can send off into the world and be proud of.

The first question that you might have is why an editor such as myself would tell you how to save money on her services. The reasons are many, but here are just a few:

1. **I am an author myself.** I plan to self-publish my own nonfiction books, novels, and short stories. I understand how big that number can look when you get an estimate from an editor to polish your manuscript. I have no desire to bankrupt writers just so they can publish books that won't send readers away screaming about errors. However, I also

know that most professional editors, myself included, charge reasonable fees with the goal of earning a comfortable living wage, but that's it. Editing has never been known as a lucrative profession.

2. **It's more enjoyable for me.** A big part of saving money on editing is sending your editor the cleanest manuscript possible. As an editor, I enjoy editing books that start out in better shape. If I'm not fixing things that it would have been easy for the author to fix on her own, I get to not only enjoy the story more but also concentrate on using the professional skills that I have spent years developing, the unique skills that authors hire me for. I have the chance to help authors make their manuscript not just good enough but extraordinary.

Like many editors, I have a range of rates that I charge for each of my services. I charge per word for fiction editing and often hourly for other work. For manuscripts that are already well polished, I charge the lower end of my per-word rate range. For manuscripts that are very messy and will take more time to clean up or analyze, I charge the upper end of that range. Currently, there is a 1.5-cent-per-word difference between my lower and upper rates for copyediting. For an author, that could mean the difference between paying me $750 to edit a well-prepared 50,000-word manuscript and paying me $1500 to edit a messy one.

3. **It won't take me as long to finish.** If your manuscript is clean, I will likely spend less time on it. I will charge you a lower per-word rate, and you will get it back faster. In the meantime, I can accept another job. So, instead of spending four weeks copyediting one messy manuscript, I can spend those same four weeks copyediting two clean ones. So, I get to read more great books and interact with more wonderful authors. It's a win–win situation.

How Patience Affects Your Editing Costs

So how, you might ask, will patience save you money on editing? When a manuscript is accepted by a publisher, it goes through a series of tried and true steps, only one of which is editing. If publishers skipped those steps, they might soon be out of business, or their reputations might suffer.

Take the same care with your own book. Be patient and hit all of the necessary steps. Make yourself a checklist of the stages that you think or know are necessary to create a great product. [You may find my post "My First Draft Is Done! What's Next? A Manuscript Guide for Indie Authors" (https://speculationsediting.com/archives/first-draft-whats-next/) helpful.] Yes, your book is a creation and a work of art, but if you want to sell it, you must also see it as a product. Makers of car seats and packaged foods pay dearly for skipping quality-assurance steps, and so do authors.

Almost everything that I will suggest to you in this book on saving money on editing will require patience, but here are a couple of guidelines that you can start with. I will cover more steps in future chapters.

1. **Don't send your first draft to an editor.** Instead, let it sit for two to three months and then self-edit it. Trust me, after you haven't laid eyes on your precious baby for a while, it won't seem as precious, and you'll be able to catch a lot of mistakes. Why pay an editor to do this part if you can do it your-

self with just a little patience and time away from your manuscript?

Does this mean that I won't take your money if you decide to send me your first draft? Of course not. When we're under contract, you are paying me to apply my skills to your book, whatever stage it's at. I can do that at any time. If you want me to start earlier in the process, I will, but I don't recommend it.

"But, Janell, what am I supposed to do? I want to publish. I can't just twiddle my thumbs for two or three months. I've got to get this baby on Amazon *now!*"

If you plan to publish only one book, you've probably been working on this book for a while. Two to three months will only make it better in the long run. For those of you who want to publish more than one novel, see point 2.

2. **Establish a cycle.** While manuscript one is stewing, start writing manuscript two. Getting all caught up in a new book is great for putting distance between you and the project that's been consuming all

of your energy for weeks (if you're a National Novel Writing Month style writer), months, or years. As an author, you also have other things that you can focus on while your brain takes a much-needed vacation from your first book, especially once you have more than one manuscript in the pipeline. You could be doing any of the following and still stay productive as a writer:

- Self-editing another manuscript.
- Preparing an edited and formatted manuscript for launch.
- Building your author platform.
- Writing a new book or short story.

3. Basically, you need to build up a write–revise–publish–promote cycle for all of your titles. Revision is not a single step. It includes self-editing, getting the help of alpha and/or beta readers, and hiring a professional editor and proofreader along with lots and lots of revision on your part. Your cycle, including revisions, might look something like this:

   a. Write first draft of Title 1.
   b. Write first draft of Title 2.

c. Self-edit Title 1.

d. Send Title 1 out to alpha readers.

e. Self-edit Title 2.

f. Send Title 2 out to alpha readers.

g. Review alpha reader feedback on Title 1 and self-edit again.

h. And on and on, working in a third or fourth title as you wish.

After you've reviewed your alpha and beta reader feedback and made any necessary changes, it might finally be a good time to start seeking a professional editor.

As with any worthwhile endeavor, you won't reach your goal overnight. You don't earn a black belt in a month, and you certainly don't become a successful, established author that quickly either, so take your time and do it right.

2. Self-Editing

In the first chapter, I covered practicing patience and the ways in which slowing down can save you, the author, money on editing.

Self-editing can also save you money, and it definitely requires some of that patience. If you are an indie author, when you complete the first draft of a book, especially your first book, you might be tempted to dive right into formatting and publishing your new book through Amazon KDP, Amazon CreateSpace, IngramSpark, Kobo Writing Life, or one of the many other avenues for self-publishing. If you are going the traditional route, you might be tempted to start sending your manuscript out to agents or publishing houses as soon as you type "The End."

By doing so, however, you are taking a dangerous gamble. Not only is your book likely to be full of typos, but it may also contain plot holes, character and plot discrepancies, contrived endings, and glaring inconsistencies that may kill the interest of readers, agents, and publishers.

As an editor, I am, of course, in favor of editing before publishing, but I am also in favor of at least two rounds of author self-editing before that professional editing takes place.

So, before you start looking for that stellar editor at just the right price, let your book sit. Fill your mind with something else for two to three months so that when you start working on it again, you are no longer seeing what you think should be on the page (a.k.a., experiencing author blindness) but instead are seeing what is actually on the page. You will be able to better see errors and inconsistencies and address them early on.

Your process might look something like this:

1. Finish the first draft.
2. Wait three months. (You could write a first draft of a new book during this time.)
3. Self-edit.
4. Send the next draft of the manuscript to volunteer readers and get feedback.
5. Self-edit according to the feedback from step 4.
6. Repeat steps 4 and 5 with alpha and beta readers until you believe that you have done as much for

the manuscript as you personally can or are willing to do without an editor's help.

7. Send the next draft of the book to an editor or editors for an evaluation to see how far you've come.

If your chosen editor recommends developmental editing (i.e., structural editing), you can work with her on this step if you're not sure what to do, or you can do another round of self-editing yourself, focusing on structural issues.

If said editor recommends copyediting, you're good to go on structural and big-picture issues and are ready to move forward.

My point here about self-editing is that by taking your time and fixing as many errors as you can with the help of readers, you can get a price on the lower end of your editor's rate range and maybe even skip structural editing altogether.

How to Make the Most of Self-Editing

Establishing a process that works well for you will take time, and it's one you'll get better at the more you write and the more you learn which steps help and which ones are a waste of time for you and your style of writing.

Some writers make many editing passes on their novel, each time looking for one specific weakness (e.g., overly used adverbs, too much telling vs showing, or inconsistencies in point of view). If this works for you, great, but I warn you: the more you read your own manuscript, the less you'll be able to really *see* it. That's author blindness kicking in again. (Editors get it, too, and that is why I recommend a separate proofreader once copyediting and formatting are finished.) Unless you want to take a year or more to finish every novel, take advantage of your alpha and beta readers to help you see the things that author blindness will, well, blind you to.

Tips for Self-Editing

Here are some tips to help you make the most of your self-editing process:

1. **Apply rules only when they actually improve the story that you want to create.** It's easy to take the many writing rules out there and apply them

universally, but thoughtlessly slashing your manu-script may cause even bigger problems.

For example, sometimes you need to tell, or summarize, less essential narrative to let the reader know what is happening so that you can get to the good stuff and really paint a vivid picture of im-portant scenes. If you overly show a less important scene and extend it to several pages, you might lose your readers' interest as they ask themselves what the point of the passage is and where the real story went.

Many authors and even some editors focus on little details that will not matter to a reader as long as the story is tight and compelling. So when you are thinking about applying a rule to your book, ask yourself, "If I saw this in a book I was reading, would it bother me?" before you jump in with the red pencil. Alternatively, you can save the original passage, make the edits you are thinking about, and then compare the two versions to see which is really better.

I know a lot of rules, but when I am editing, especially for big-picture issues, I read like a reader first. When my brain tells me that something doesn't feel right or is just awkward or boring, it is only then that I get down to the nitty-gritty details and dissect the manuscript to see why it doesn't work. Don't waste time worrying that you overused a certain word or type of word until your alpha or beta readers point it out or you yourself are bothered by it when reviewing your manuscript.

2. **Start with the big-picture items first and then move to the smaller details.** By big-picture items, I mean plot, characterization, structure, overall consistency, timelines and chronologies, tone, theme, and flow. By smaller details, I mean spelling, grammar, punctuation, capitalization, word choice, and consistency in the details. (Yes, there are different types of consistency, and they are all important to editing.)

As you're self-editing, if you see a spelling mistake, it's okay to fix it, but don't get bogged down in the little details until the overarching structure has been addressed. You might end up deleting that sentence or passage later anyway. So, address the big picture first: How are your structure and pacing? Does your story compel the reader ever forward, ever faster in a race to an intense, surprising, inevitable climax? Are the arcs of your main characters complete? Does your timeline make sense, or are your flashbacks confusing your readers? Does your dialog sound natural for each character, or is it stilted? Are your characters' accents overdone and pulling your reader out of the story?

Only when you and your volunteer readers are sure that the story is in good shape should you start to worry about the rest.

3. **Take advantage of free and low-cost resources.** Any Google search will tell you that there are many, many free blog posts and articles out there to help you with self-editing. There will be a vast number of opinions on the best way to go about self-editing. I recommend that you find a few writing experts online that gel with your own ideas about writing and use them to help you figure out what to

look for and what to focus on during your editing process. Some of my favorite resources are *Writing Excuses* (podcast, http://www.writingexcuses.com/), *Helping Writers Become Authors* (blog, https://www.helpingwritersbecomeauthors.com/), *Writer Unboxed* (blog, http://writerunboxed.com/), *Fiction University* (blog, http://blog.janicehardy.com/), *Writer's Digest* (website and blogs, http://www.writersdigest.com/), and *This Itch of Writing* (blog, http://emmadarwin.typepad.com/).

Another source of inexpensive guidance is the library of books available on Amazon's Kindle Unlimited. I have found a multitude of titles on the writing craft available to borrow with my subscription.

Other Resources for Self-Editing

Here are some resources that I have found particularly helpful. I have a more extensive, updated list of resources for fiction writers (https://speculationsediting.com/writing-resources-for-fiction-writers/) on my website.

- Renni Browne and Dave King, *Self-Editing for Fiction Writers: How to Edit Yourself Into Print* (https://www.amazon.com/Self-Editing-Fiction-Writers-Second-Yourself/dp/0060545690/), 2nd ed. (New York: William Morrow, 2004).

- Beth Hill, "Checklist for Editors" (http://theeditorsblog.net/2011/06/07/checklist-for-editors/), *The Editor's Blog* (blog), June 7, 2011.

- Emma Darwin, "The Fiction Editor's Pharmacopoeia; Diagnosing Symptoms & Treating the Disease" (http://emmadarwin.typepad.com/thisitchofwriting/2016/06/the-fiction-editors-pharmacopoeia-diagnosing-treating-symptoms.html), *This Itch of Writing* (blog), June 13, 2016.

- Emma Darwin, "How Do You Eat an Elephant?" (http://emmadarwin.typepad.com/thisitchofwriting/2011/06/how-to-eat-an-elephant.html), *This Itch of Writing* (blog), June 23, 2011.

- K. M. Weiland, "How I Self-Edit My Novels: 15 Steps From First Draft to Publication" (http://www.helpingwritersbecomeauthors.com/ho

w-i-self-edit-my-novels-15-steps-from/), *Helping Writers Become Authors* (blog), June 9, 2013.

- Janice Hardy, "How to Be Your Own Book Doctor" (http://blog.janicehardy.com/2013/03/be-your-own-book-doctor.html), *Fiction University* (blog), December 9, 2012.

In the next chapter, I'll cover alpha and beta readers and critique partners in more depth with a little more information on how to find them and use them to your advantage in getting your book ready for professional editing.

3. Using Readers

In this chapter, I cover how you can use readers to save money on editing, and I offer you a few tips on how to find them.

Why You Need Readers

If you are a career-track author, you should use a professional editor, one who is trained to help you with certain aspects of your manuscript. However, an editor is still only one person. It would be cool to be able to hire a team of editors, but most of us can't afford that. If an editor is given a first draft and asked to turn it into a structurally sound, grammatically clean, marketable manuscript, there are many more stages for her to go through to get to the end product than if she starts with a third or fourth draft.

So, instead of giving your editor your first draft, let your readers help you suss out as many problems as you can before you hand it over. When your manuscript is in better condition, your editor can take it further, and a cleaner initial manuscript means lower rates.

What Kinds of Readers Do You Need?

Despite popular belief, authors do not have to be solely responsible for the fate of their ideas. There are many people who can help them as they turn those ideas into fully fledged books. Professional editors are among the last in line. Before them are volunteer or paid readers.

I am not going to tell you which kinds of readers to use and in what order. You can choose just one type or all of them. Each writer has a different process that works well for her. Some authors crave the reinforcement of reader feedback as they build a manuscript (alpha readers), while others prefer not to have that outside influence until their manuscript is more solid and complete (beta readers).

However, I do recommend that you get feedback on your complete manuscript from at least one reader whom you trust before you show it to your editor. This reader should be someone who is familiar with the genre and with what makes writing interesting and engaging. You may find that a mix of "just readers" and writers provides a good balance of feedback because of their different perspectives on the craft.

Personally, I sometimes show chapters of my own writing to my critique group as I write. However, I prefer a round of self-editing before I get outside feedback on any of my manuscripts as a whole. In any case, my work will have seen at least two rounds of revisions/self-editing and usually two rounds of reader feedback before I send it to my editor.

Please note: It may be a bit of a process to find readers who are dependable and who can give you the kind of feedback that you need. If you find good readers, cherish them, pay them in chocolate, and use them whenever they are willing to help you.

ALPHA READERS

Alpha readers are your first readers. They read the manuscript as it is created or once the first draft is complete. If your alpha readers agree, you can send them your manuscript a chapter at a time as you write, and you can modify your work as you continue on the basis of their feedback.

BETA READERS

Beta readers see the manuscript after it is complete and usually after at least one round of self-editing. Beta readers are people who read books. They are your test audience and can be anyone from your grandma to your friends from work to online group members.

Because beta readers are like a pilot audience, make sure that your betas regularly read books in your genre. They will be less impressed by the newness of your subject matter and will be more likely to give you feedback that you can use in the competitive marketplace that is book publishing. They will also be less likely to give you advice that it is irrelevant to your area of writing.

Most beta readers are free, but you can find paid beta readers or get paid manuscript critiques or manuscript evaluations from editors as well. This may not save you a ton of money, but it should guarantee that your readers finish your manuscript and get it back to you in a timely fashion (which many beta readers fail to do).

CRITIQUE PARTNERS

Critique partners are other writers with whom you exchange pieces of writing regularly for feedback. It's a tit-for-tat system of "if you read mine, I'll read yours." Unlike typical alpha and beta readers, your critique partner has a vested interested in helping you out because she wants you to read and comment on her manuscript as well. She has also had the experience of writing and hopefully even studying the craft more than your average alpha or beta reader.

CRITIQUE GROUPS

Online or in-person critique groups can be a great place to not only get feedback but also learn to give it. A great critique group can carry you through various stages in your writing career, but with any group, online or in person, take your time to get to know the group and make sure that it fits your style and your goals before submitting your own work. You may find that the feedback you get, especially in random online groups, is too harsh to use effectively or that some people are there to troll you or give you negative feedback just because they can.

Where to Find Readers

CRITIQUE GROUPS AND PARTNERS

To find writing groups, check your local newspaper, do online searches ("writers' groups near me"), or start your own. I found my critique group through a statewide writers' club that has chapters throughout my state.

Writers and Editors lists many groups on its website (http://www.writersandeditors.com/).

Even if your local or online writing group doesn't do critiques, once you get to know people, you might be able to find others in the group willing to exchange writing with you on an individual basis, and thus, a critique partnership might be born!

ALPHA AND BETA READERS

Use friends, family, and coworkers, but choose carefully. Your readers should be the kind of people who aren't afraid to tell you what they *really* think. Kudos aren't critical feedback, and they won't make your book better.

You can find alpha and beta readers through online or in-person writing groups (see Critique Groups and Partners).

A couple of simple searches will show that there are many beta reader groups on both Goodreads and Facebook. Also, K. M. Weiland at *Helping Writers Become Authors* (https://www.helpingwritersbecomeauthors.com/) put together a handy list of places to find beta readers (https://www.helpingwritersbecomeauthors.com/find-your-next-beta-reader/).

Resources

Because the subject of getting feedback from beta readers and others could be a whole book in itself, here are a few other resources to help you out:

- Mary Robinette Kowal, "How and Why I Use Online Alpha-Readers While Writing Novels" (http://maryrobinettekowal.com/journal/how-and-why-i-use-online-alpha-readers-while-writing-novels/), *Mary Robinette Kowal* (blog), November 28, 2012.

- Kristen Kieffer, "How to Find and Work with Beta Readers to Improve Your Book" (http://janefriedman.com/find-beta-readers/), *JaneFriedman.com*, January 18, 2016.

- K. M. Weiland, "How to Find the Right Critique Partner: The 6-Step Checklist" (http://www. helpingwritersbecomeauthors.com/how-to-find-the-right-critique-partner/), *Helping Writers Become Authors* (blog), August 15, 2016.

- Janice Hardy, "Should You Have an Alpha Reader?" (http://blog.janicehardy.com/2015/04/should-you-have-alpha-reader.html), *Fiction University* (blog), April 13, 2015.

- Valerie Peterson, "To Help Get Your Novel Published—Use Reader Feedback Wisely" (http://www. thebalance.com/publishing-novel-reader-feedback-2799870), *the balance,* January 31, 2016.

- Jen Anderson, "The Importance and Limitations of Beta Readers" (http://www.clearingblocksediting.com/the-importance-and-limitations-of-beta-readers/), *Clearing Blocks*

4. Using Editing Tools

So far we've talked about how practicing patience, self-editing, and using readers can help you produce a cleaner manuscript and reduce your editing costs. In this chapter, I cover a topic that makes me cringe—editing tools—but I can't ignore them. They're out there, and authors are going to use them. I just hope my tips can help writers use them smartly.

Why do electronic editing tools make me cringe? Because editing tools, such as our old friend the spell checker, can become your enemy very quickly if they are used in the wrong way. The Replace All feature can quickly ruin a good manuscript. There are too many exceptions in the English language to make the broad application of nearly any "rule" a good idea.

An electronic tool can make suggestions but cannot interpret everything in context and cannot tell you whether a change actually works for your manuscript. Tools can definitely make life easier, but their use requires a deep understanding of our language and the rules of writing and grammar that govern it. If you don't already understand them (as your editor should), you may end up introducing more errors into your manuscript than you correct.

So, before I list some of the tools out there that you might find useful for cleaning up your manuscript, I'd like to offer a few words of caution:

- Always check each suggested change carefully before accepting it.

- If you don't know why a change is being suggested, look it up. You might learn something new, or you might learn that the particular suggestion doesn't apply to your manuscript.

- Some of these tools and apps give feedback on readability. Consider carefully what level of readability is appropriate for your work before making any suggested changes. Not every manuscript or blog post needs to be readable at a third-grade reading level or whatever baseline level the tool uses.

What about the Costs?

Most of these tools cost money. However, if you use a favorite on multiple manuscripts, the per-book investment for most of these tools could turn out to be very small, depending on your writing output. Many of these tools come with a free trial, so if you're curious, you can check them out before you hand over your money.

If you choose your apps judiciously, you can use them to produce cleaner manuscripts for your editor and hopefully reduce your overall editing costs a little bit. If you use apps together, you will cover more ground and probably also see some overlapping functions.

Keep in mind that these software applications are not meant to serve as replacements for an actual editor.

Notable Editing Tools

I have chosen tools suggested to me by other editors and ones that will be particularly useful for fiction and/or creative nonfiction writers. This list is not exhaustive. There are even more tools out there for academic, technical, and other specialty writers. As always, do your research.

Always save a backup of your manuscript before you run any tool, and understand that you use it at your own risk.

WORD ADD-ONS

- **PerfectIt Pro (available at http://www. intelligentediting.com/):** I have used this Word add-on for years. It is a customizable tool that can be used to help you add consistency to your use of words, phrases, and form (e.g., Oxford commas). It will flag instances of inconsistencies (unstoppable vs. un-stoppable) and style deviations and give you a chance to easily correct them. You can also use and create customizable style sheets if you do more than one kind of writing. It is hard to cover it all in a paragraph, but I have found this tool to be well worth the investment.

- **Editorium Add-Ons (especially the Editor's ToolKit and File Cleaner, available at http:// www.editorium.com/):** According to Editorium's website, the Editor's ToolKit "provides powerful tools for editing in Microsoft Word, including the ability to show and stet revisions at the touch of a key. Quickly transpose words, transpose characters, change case, and so on. Editor's ToolKit makes editing in Microsoft Word an absolute pleasure." File Cleaner focuses more on correcting common mechanical mistakes, such as too many spaces or improperly typed characters. A good knowledge of Word macros is recommended here. Unfortunately, in my trial run of these macros, I quickly discovered some bugs, although they might have been due to version incompatibility.

- **SmartEdit (available at http://www.smart-edit.**

  com/): This tool's makers describe it as a "first-pass editing tool for creative writers and novelists that sits inside Microsoft Word and helps you as you work…. It's an aid—a helper for when you begin editing your work. A stand-alone version also exists for writers who do not use Word." It highlights things such as adverbs, repeated words and phrases, and clichés so that you can change them if you wish.

STAND-ALONE AND MULTI-INTEGRATING TOOLS

- **ProWritingAid (available at https://prowritingaid. com/):** Similar to SmartEdit, this tool promises to help writers improve their writing through checks that flag things such as repeated words and adverb use. It also "integrates with MS Word, Open Office, Google Docs, Scrivener and Google Chrome."

- **Hemingway App (available at http://www. hemingwayapp.com/):** Through the creative use of highlighting, this tool seeks to help you improve the clarity and readability of your writing.

- **Grammarly (available at https://www. grammarly.com/):** This app has free and paid versions and can be used not only as a Word add-on but also in your browser or as a Windows application. As its name suggests, it focuses on grammar and touts itself as far better than Word's built-in spelling and grammar checkers. I used Grammarly for a while to see whether it could add robustness to my own editing and writing through extra checks. However, I found that the number of false-positive results and the fact that you cannot save items you've already checked in a document made it more trouble for me than it was worth, especially for very long books.

5. Final Tips

By now you've figured out that the whole point of this book is that you can save money on editing by providing your editor with a cleaner, more developed manuscript. In this post, I include more tips to help you get that cleaner manuscript and some tips that fall outside this realm.

Improve Your Own Skills

How are your own writing skills? If there is one thing that I have learned as a published author and as an editor of almost twenty years, it's that there are always new things to learn and new ways of getting better at my craft. With the following steps, you can work on improving your own writing and self-editing skills so that each work you produce is better than the last:

1. **Learn more about the writing craft.** Read books, listen to podcasts, watch videos, and attend workshops, conferences, and critique groups. Learn all

you can about story structure, theme, plot, characterization, and so on. I have a growing list of resources of all kinds (podcasts, audiobooks, videos, and reading materials) on the resources for fiction writers page (https://speculationsediting.com/writing-resources-for-fiction-writers/) on my website.

2. **Learn more about grammar.** Pick up a book such as the *Blue Book of Grammar* (http://www.grammarbook.com/) by Jane Straus, Lester Kaufman, and Tom Stern or *Say What?: The Fiction Writer's Handy Guide to Grammar, Punctuation, and Word Usage* (https://www.amazon.com/Say-What-Fiction-Writers-Punctuation/dp/0986134708) by C. S. Lakin and polish your skills. In the process, you will be learning why editors make many of the changes that we do. Keep these books handy: you will refer to them over and over again. Your knowledge from your high school or college English class will not be enough. There is so much more to learn.

3. **Think about consistency during the self-editing stage.** One of the biggest things that editors look

for is consistency. So if you realize that you keep changing the spelling of a character's name or the capitalization of a phrase, use the handy search and replace tool in your word processor to check for these errors. Highlight "pet" words or phrases that you tend to repeat a lot (trust me, all writers have them).

4. **Use a style manual.** Why? Readers like consistency. Inconsistencies pull them out of the story and disrupt their ability to enjoy it. Style manuals give you rules that help you to maintain consistency throughout your manuscript and provide guidelines for correct grammar, spelling, and punctuation. Most fiction editors use the *Chicago Manual of Style*. The 16th edition is available online (http://www.chicagomanualofstyle.org/home.html) and in print (https://www.amazon.com/Chicago-Manual-Style-16th/dp/0226104206), and the 17th edition (https://www.amazon.com/Chicago-Manual-Style-17th/dp/022628705X) is forthcoming as I write this. Not only can you use this manual to make your own style decisions, but you will also have it nearby

when your editor inevitably quotes a section of the manual when explaining certain editorial changes.

Practice Smart Shopping

If you are interested in saving money on editing, when you shop for an editor, there are a few more things that you can do while still getting a professional edit:

1. **Comparison shop.** Find a directory of editors that you trust. I recommend the directories of the Editorial Freelancers Association (http://www.the-efa.org/dir/) in the United States and the Society for Editors and Proofreaders (https://www.sfep.org.uk/directory/) in the United Kingdom. Find a few editors that work on your type of book and request sample edits and estimates. Use this information to pick the best editor you can at the best price.

2. **Look for deals.** If your editor doesn't list these on her website, feel free to ask.

   a. **Does your editor offer package deals?** If you are self-publishing, you may need several services, such as developmental editing, copyediting, and formatting. Many editors offer packages, sometimes with other service providers, to save money. They provide convenience by allowing authors to get many or all of their needs handled in one place.

b. **Does your editor offer trimmed-down versions of services?** For example, you might get a manuscript evaluation or a three-chapter critique instead of a full developmental edit. You might find that you can extrapolate the feedback your editor gives you on a shorter section to your entire book.

3. **Barter.** If you have marketable skills, it never hurts to ask your editor if there is something that you can offer in trade for editing. Perhaps you could trade web design skills, marketing services, or social media help for editing. If you know an editor in person, you could even offer more tangible skills. For example, I provide publishing consulting services to

a local musician/author in exchange for my daughter's piano lessons. It all works out very well.

A Note on Cheap Editing

You'll notice that nowhere do I recommend that you find the cheapest editor possible. There are websites and forums where people offer up editing services at extremely low prices.

I am against this primarily because it lowers the value of editing in general, and editors need to make a living. An editor may spend 60–80 hours editing your manuscript. Editing is not just a one-pass reading of your book. It is deeper and requires multiple passes and extensive knowledge. Would it be fair for this editor to be paid a total of only $100 for this time? *That is less than $1.50 an hour!* Sure, some editors may agree to this, especially if they are trying to build their portfolios, but they are pricing other editors— editors with decades of experience who invest in their careers through continued training and education—right out of the market.

Unfortunately, there is no universal certification for editors, one that would guarantee that you are getting a professional editor with the kind of experience you need.

As a result, when authors hire cheap editors, they may be hiring people who simply did well in college English and feel that they are qualified to call themselves editors. These people often provide shoddy work. Stories of these experiences spread like wildfire over the internet, and pretty soon, everyone thinks that all freelance editors are scam artists.

So, do your research.

When hiring any editor, you must vet the editor carefully through questions about her background and experience, the books and other publications she has edited, her relevant education, and her professional certifications and memberships. Get a sample edit to make sure that your styles mesh and that her skills are on par. See if it would be possible for you to correspond with a past client or two so that you can find out what their experiences were.

Again, do your research, and you are less likely to get burned. In the following bonus section, I explain how to do just that.

6. Finding Your Best Editor

In this chapter, I discuss the process of vetting editors. At the end of the last chapter, I mentioned cheap editing and why I am against it. One of the reasons is that self-published authors often get scammed by people who claim that they are editors, even though they have no training or education in editing.

As Cheryl of Ink Slinger Editorial Services (http://inkslingereditorialservices.com/) puts it, "The hardest thing about finding an editor is that anyone can hang a shingle. Especially someone that says they made *As* in high school English and loves to read. Editing is a skill. Accept that it's a skill, and you'll find a proper editor. And remember that being a writer does not qualify you to be an editor, either."

So, as a follow-up to the previous chapters, I want to give you some information on how you can vet your freelance editor and make sure that you get what you pay for and that you get an editor who is a good match for you. If you produce more than one book, this could be a relationship that lasts for years.

Keep in mind that when you are vetting editors, not every editor will hit every point on this list. However, if you examine them all, you will get a good feel for just how professional and experienced your editor is. In many cases, she will already have most of this information available for you on her website or resume.

Alternately, an editor who is lacking in all or many of these areas might not be your best choice.

Before You Start Vetting

Don't waste your time vetting an editor only to find out that there is no way she can edit your book or do it wisely. Make sure to check in with her first and find out:

1. **Is the editor available when you need her to be?** Many freelance editors are booked months (sometimes years) in advance. As editor Averill Buchanan (http://www.averillbuchanan.com/) says, there is not much point in spending valuable time vetting someone who won't be available on your schedule. For a good editor, however, you might find yourself

willing to accept a spot on her editorial calendar that is months away.

2. **Is this person the right kind of editor?** There are seemingly a million jobs out there with the title *editor*, all with different job descriptions. Check the editor's website or ask her straight out what kind of editor she is and make sure that she provides the kind of editing you are looking for.

Simply put, if your story needs structural work, you need a developmental editor. If the grammar needs to be checked, you need a copyeditor or line editor. If you need someone to check your final, formatted pages for errors, you need a proofreader.

Some editors provide all of these services plus others, such as consulting or cover design. Diversification can be a savvy business practice in today's market. However, some editors provide only one kind of service on one kind of book. Make sure that you get the right one.

Education

Now it's time to start researching your editor to find out if she has the qualifications you are looking for in a publishing professional. There are many things to look at. Let's start with education. There are different ways to measure this when it comes to editorial professionals:

1. **Degree or Certificate.** Does the editor have a relevant degree or certificate in publishing or editing? This shows you that the person has spent some time learning the craft.

   Keep in mind that many editors do not have an editing degree or a certificate because they got their start in publishing houses, where they received on-the-job training before they went independent. Some freelance editors may also still be working in house and providing independent services in their off-hours. That's how I got my start.

2. **Continuing Education.** There are many courses available to editors through the Editorial Freelancers Association (http://www.the-efa.org/eve/education. php), the Society for Editors and Proofreaders

(https://www.sfep.org.uk/training/), and Copyediting.com (https://www.copyediting.com/individual-training/master-classes/) and from other sources. Has your prospective editor taken advantage of one or more of these courses to keep her skills up to date or perhaps to expand her editing skill set into a new area?

Your editor may have many or only a few of these courses under her belt. If her editorial calendar has been full, she may not have made time for classes. On the other hand, natural gaps in the editorial calendar can provide some time for editors to keep their skills up to date.

Relevant Experience

Relevant experience not only complements education but is probably even more important.

As Susan Wenger of Cover to Cover (http://covertocoverllc.com/) says, "Ask your prospective editor about relevant experience. If the *only* thing they tell you is that they have an English degree, or they teach English/literature, run. These things can be helpful, but they're not sufficient."

While exploring your prospective editor's experience, here are some things to look for:

1. **General Editing Experience.** How long has the editor been working professionally? Has she ever worked in house for a legitimate publisher? How many hours per week does she generally spend editing?

2. **Specific Editing Experience.** Does the editor have experience working in your field? This can be as broad as fiction versus nonfiction but can reach all the way down to a specific genre, such as paranormal romance. Ask for a list of books in your area that she has worked on.

You might also ask about the editor's favorite books in your genre. A love of a certain type of book obviously doesn't stand in for editing skill. However, when an editor brings years of editing experience to the table plus a deep knowledge of your genre, she will be able to recognize the tropes and conventions of the type of book you want to write and help you create a more marketable manuscript.

If the editor does not have a lot of experience in your genre or niche but has a lot of general experience and you feel good about your communication so far, look to her continuing education, author testimonials, and sample edit to determine her competence.

Process

Find out how the editor works and how she likes to communicate. Finding someone compatible can save you lots of frustration down the line:

- Does she edit in a program that is compatible with your own (usually Word)?
- Does she use Track Changes or an equivalent tool that makes it easy for you to see edits and accept or reject them?
- How many passes does each round of editing include?
- Does your prospective editor prefer Skype, phone, or email to communicate?

- Do her rates include a reasonable amount of time for you to respond or ask questions about the editing after it is complete?

Professionalism

Through your initial communication and research, find out if the editor behaves in a professional manner:

- Does she respond to you in a timely manner?
- Does she respond professionally to a reasonable number of questions?
- Is she respectful to you? Does she treat you like a professional?
- Does she offer a written contract for her services? If she doesn't, move on. A contract protects you both.
- Does she recognize your ownership over your content (i.e., your authority to make the last call on all editing decisions)?
- Is she a member of a relevant professional organization such as the Editorial Freelancers Association,

the Society for Editors and Proofreaders, or the Association of Independent Publishing Professionals?

Internet/Social Media Presence

In the process of vetting editors, it is a good idea to check out each editor's web presence. If an editor is a professional, it is likely that she has established herself on the Internet to increase her discoverability, just as authors often do. Check out her various footprints to get an idea about who she is and what services she offers. If you find an editor in a Goodreads forum but nowhere else on the web, there's a good chance that she hasn't been editing for long or at all. Here are some good questions to ask yourself as you investigate:

- Does she have a website? Is it professional in appearance, and does it give you answers to many of the questions listed in this post?
- Is she on social media in a professional capacity (e.g., is her business on Twitter, Facebook, Instagram, or LinkedIn)? You can get some idea of an

editor's professional interactions through how she presents herself on social media.

Past Clients

When you're vetting editors for your book, perhaps the most important step is to find out what their previous clients have to say:

1. **Look for testimonials.** Like all people, editors like to share when they have received praise for a job well done. They will often have testimonials from past clients and colleagues posted on their websites. See if it is possible for you to speak to past clients so you can get an idea of how each editor works and how satisfied her clients have been.

2. **Ask your author friends for recommendations.** You may find that your fellow authors can tell you about the good, the bad, and the ugly with respect to editors that they have worked with. Consider their opinions cautiously, but don't dismiss them. If an author has glowing praise for her editor, take a closer look and judge for yourself.

Sample the Service

Most editors will offer a free sample edit of some length. Mine is 1250 words, and other editors may offer more or less. The sample edit allows both you and the editor to learn a bit about each other's styles and see if you are a good fit. The editor can also use the sample edit to determine how much work is needed on your manuscript so that she can come up with a proper estimate.

Take advantage of this. When you find a few editors that are serious contenders, get sample edits and estimates from each one. It will be extremely helpful not only for vetting the editors but also for choosing the one that you want to work with most.

Upfront Payments

In this age of constant scams, authors aren't the only ones who are wary. Editors must also be careful about putting in weeks' worth of work on a manuscript only to be left high and dry when the work is done. So, to protect their own interests, many editors ask for a deposit upfront and the rest of the payment for their services before you get your edited manuscript back.

So, to keep yourself from being left with no money and a sloppily edited book (or no book at all), do your research, and vet your editors appropriately. Talk to their past clients and make sure that they are legitimate. Keep in mind that no one with experience and an established Internet presence can scam her clients for long without getting numerous public responses. Let the editor's reputation speak for itself. If it doesn't, you have to decide if it's a risk you are willing to take. (Again, this is a great topic to speak with past clients about.)

Thanks

I had some help from fellow editors with this chapter so that I could provide you with a thorough list of steps for vetting editors. In that capacity, I'd like to thank Susan Wenger (http://covertocoverllc.com/), Averill Buchanan (http://www.averillbuchanan.com/), Cheryl Murphy Lowrance (http://inkslingereditorialservices.com/), Janet MacMillan (http://www.janetmacmillanwordsmith.com/), Julia Ganis, (http://juliaedits.com/), and Dorothy Zemach (https://

www.linkedin.com/in/dorothyzemach) for their input and insights.

Note from the Author

I have used the pronouns she and her to refer to single authors or editors throughout this book. However, this is just for simplicity. There are many fine authors and editors out there who are not female.

I hope that you have enjoyed this book, and I welcome your feedback and tips for future editions. If you did, I encourage you to leave a review on Goodreads or Amazon and let other readers know what you liked about it!

Free Self-Editing Checklist for Your First Draft

If you liked this book and would like to receive a free comprehensive checklist for self-editing your first draft, please sign up for my mailing list at http://eepurl.com/cJwLXD. You will also receive more information on writing and self-publishing, including when the next book in this series is released. I only email when there is something new (a blog post, book, or new resources) to share!

About the Author

The owner of Speculations Editing Services (https://
speculationsediting.com/) and Robisch Editorial Services
(the academic branch of her business), Janell is a published
author and independent editor with more than 20 years of
experience in the publishing industry and more than 15
years of experience as a full-time, independent editor.

Janell began her career in publishing by working for an
author in college. Later, she worked for several publishers,
including Oxford University Press and Lawrence Erlbaum
Associates. In 2001, she began her current career as a full-
time independent editor and later added book formatting
and cover design to her portfolio.

Janell regularly publishes posts on writing and publishing on her blog, *Wordy Speculations* (https://speculationsediting.
com/wordy-speculations/).

She also writes fiction under the pen name J. Elizabeth
Vincent and is the facilitator of a satellite group of the Vir-
ginia Writers Club, a board member for her local communi-

ty theater, and a member of the Editorial Freelancers Association.

But most of all, she's a wife and a mother to three kids. Her family has lots of adventures together, homeschooling and following all of their various passions in life, which to this point have included writing, karate, medieval longsword training, gymnastics, dance, piano, singing, art, and many, many, many video games.

Where to Find Janell Online

Web: https://speculationsediting.com

Facebook: https://www.facebook.com/speculationsediting

Twitter: https://twitter.com/Fiction_Editor

Editorial Freelancers Association: http://www.the-efa. org/dir/memberinfo.php?mid=17737

LinkedIn: https://www.linkedin.com/in/janell-robisch/

Acknowledgments

Janell would like to thank her family for their endless patience with all of the hours that she spends in front of the computer screen writing, editing, and researching.

In particular, she would like to thank her husband, Alan, for his endless support of her pursuits and all of the free editing that he provides (yes, he's a professional editor, too).